Dear Parents and Educators,

Welcome to Penguin Young Readers! As parents and educators, you know that each child develops at his or her own pace—in terms of speech, critical thinking, and, of course, reading. Penguin Young Readers recognizes this fact. As a result, each Penguin Young Readers book is assigned a traditional easy-to-read level (1–4) as well as a Guided Reading Level (A–P). Both of these systems will help you choose the right book for your child. Please refer to the back of each book for specific leveling information. Penguin Young Readers features esteemed authors and illustrators, stories about favorite characters, fascinating nonfiction, and more!

## Why Do Dogs Bark?

LEVEL **3**

GUIDED READING LEVEL **L**

This book is perfect for a **Transitional Reader** who:
- can read multisyllable and compound words;
- can read words with prefixes and suffixes;
- is able to identify story elements (beginning, middle, end, plot, setting, characters, problem, solution); and
- can understand different points of view.

Here are some **activities** you can do during and after reading this book:
- Comprehension: Answer the following questions about dogs.
  - What do you call a group of puppies born at the same time?
  - How do dogs cool off when they are hot?
  - Why are Saint Bernards so good at finding people lost in snowstorms?
  - Who was Balto?
- Make Connections: We find out in this book that some dogs can learn 20 or more words. Think about the dogs you know. What words do they understand? How can you tell?

Remember, sharing the love of reading with a child is the best gift you can give!

—Bonnie Bader, EdM
  Penguin Young Readers program

*Penguin Young Readers are leveled by independent reviewers applying the standards developed by Irene Fountas and Gay Su Pinnell in *Matching Books to Readers: Using Leveled Books in Guided Reading*, Heinemann, 1999.

With thanks to Joy and Dena,
my wonderful editors

Thanks to Stephen Zawistowski, PhD,
Certified Applied Animal Behaviorist,
for his help—JH

For Michael and Stephen Olinger—AD

Penguin Young Readers
Published by the Penguin Group
Penguin Group (USA) Inc., 375 Hudson Street, New York, New York 10014, USA
Penguin Group (Canada), 90 Eglinton Avenue East, Suite 700, Toronto, Ontario M4P 2Y3, Canada
(a division of Pearson Penguin Canada Inc.)
Penguin Books Ltd., 80 Strand, London WC2R 0RL, England
Penguin Group Ireland, 25 St. Stephen's Green, Dublin 2, Ireland (a division of Penguin Books Ltd.)
Penguin Group (Australia), 250 Camberwell Road, Camberwell, Victoria 3124, Australia
(a division of Pearson Australia Group Pty. Ltd.)
Penguin Books India Pvt. Ltd., 11 Community Centre, Panchsheel Park, New Delhi—110 017, India
Penguin Group (NZ), 67 Apollo Drive, Rosedale, Auckland 0632, New Zealand
(a division of Pearson New Zealand Ltd.)
Penguin Books (South Africa) (Pty.) Ltd., 24 Sturdee Avenue,
Rosebank, Johannesburg 2196, South Africa

Penguin Books Ltd., Registered Offices: 80 Strand, London WC2R 0RL, England

Photo credits: front cover, pages 7, 9 (Australian Shepherd, Mixed Breed, and Boston Terrier),
25, 33, 45 © Davis/Lynn Images; pages 1, 5 (Golden Retriever), 10, 11, 14 (two wolves—D. Robert Franz),
15 (Rita Summers), 18, 21, 23, 36–39, 48 © Ron Kimball Studios; pages 13, 34 © Elizabeth Hathon.

The Library of Congress has cataloged the Dial edition under the following Control Number: 00023984

ISBN 978-0-14-056789-2

# Why Do Dogs Bark?

by Joan Holub
illustrations by Anna DiVito
and with photographs

Penguin Young Readers
An Imprint of Penguin Group (USA) Inc.

# Do you love dogs?

Many people love dogs. Dogs are even called "man's best friend."

There are over 100 kinds, or breeds, of pet dogs.

Some popular breeds are retrievers (say: ree-TREE-vurz), cocker spaniels, poodles, beagles, Rottweilers (say: ROT-wy-lerz), and German shepherds.

Dogs that are a mix of breeds are called mixed-breeds or mutts.

# Which dogs are smallest and biggest?

Dogs come in many different shapes and sizes.

Chihuahuas (say: chuh-WAH-waz) are the smallest dogs. A Teacup Chihuahua will fit in your hand.

Mastiffs and Saint Bernards are the biggest dogs. They can weigh over 250 pounds. That is about as much as four kids your age!

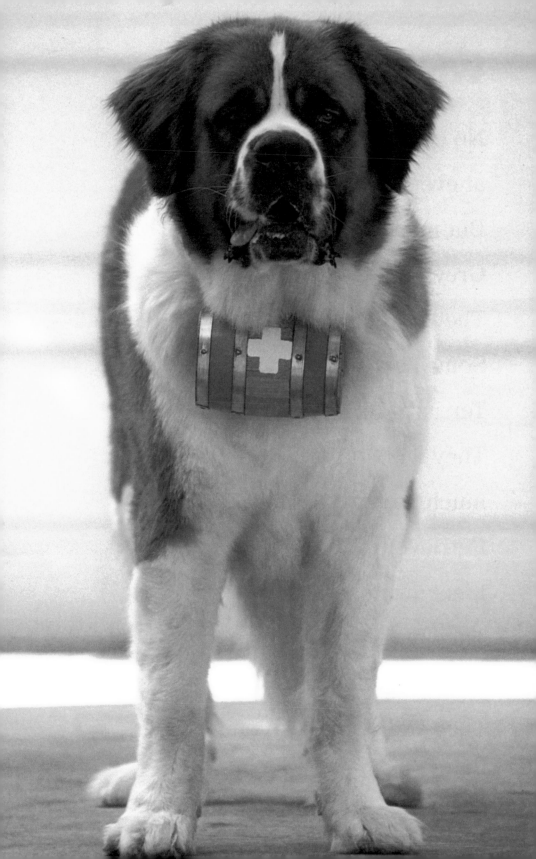

# Which dogs are best?

No one breed of dog is best at everything. But many breeds have special skills.

Greyhounds can run very fast. They have powerful legs and thin bodies. Some can run 40 miles an hour.

Terriers (say: TER-ee-urz) are brave. They will hunt animals that are much larger than they are.

Retrievers are great swimmers. They have webbed toes to help them swim. They can even swim underwater.

What can your dog do best?

# How many puppies can a dog have at one time?

A group of puppies born at one time is called a litter. A mother dog can have many puppies in one litter.

Five is the most common number.

One dog had a litter of 22 puppies!
Newborn puppies of all breeds
look a lot alike. It can be hard to tell
what breed a newborn puppy is.

# How does a puppy grow up to be a dog?

Puppies are born with their eyes closed. They can't see or hear until they are two to three weeks old.

When puppies are three to four weeks old, they begin to walk, bark, play, and wag their tails.

Puppies drink milk from their mothers until they are five to seven weeks old. They may also lick their mother's face so she'll spit up food for them to eat.

Then they are usually ready to eat puppy food.

Most puppies become full-grown dogs when they are one year old.

# Are dogs related to wolves?

Yes! A long time ago, there were no dogs. Then people taught some wolves to be helpful.

Over hundreds of years, some of these wolves changed. They became the dogs we have today. Other wolves did not change. They are still wild.

# What is a pack of dogs or wolves?

A pack is like a dog's family.

Dogs and wolves like to eat, play, and sleep with their pack.

Each pack has one leader. Your dog thinks your family is its pack. It thinks someone in your family is the leader.

Do you know who?

# Why do dogs bark?

Your dog barks to protect your house and yard.

When a stranger comes around, it barks to sound an alarm. It wants to tell you and your family that a stranger is nearby.

Your dog may also bark to tell a stranger to go away.

Some dogs bark to greet their owners when they come home.

# Why do dogs howl?

Some dogs howl when they are lonely.

If your dog is alone for too long, it may howl. It is trying to find you or its dog friends. Other dogs may howl back to say hello.

Some dogs howl when they hear singing, music, or sirens. They think it sounds like other dogs howling, so they want to howl back.

# Why do dogs bury bones?

Dogs and wolves almost always want to eat.

Wolves must work hard to find food. They eat fast, before other animals can steal their food. That is where the saying "wolf it down" comes from.

When wolves have extra food, they bury it to save it for later.

Pet dogs also worry that someone will take their food. So they eat fast, too. Some pet dogs bury or hide bones to save them for later.

Does your dog do this?

# Can dogs see better than people?

Dogs can see better than people can at night. They are also better at seeing movement from far away.

But dogs do not see colors very well. They can see the color blue. But most other colors look gray to a dog.

# Can dogs hear better than people?

Yes! Dogs can hear high tones and soft sounds that people can't hear.

You can't hear the high sound of a dog whistle, but your dog can.

Dogs can also tell which direction a sound is coming from better than you can.

# Why do dogs sniff you?

Smell is a dog's most important sense.

A dog's sense of smell is over 100 times better than your sense of smell.

A dog sniffs you to find out who you are. It can probably tell if you are afraid by how you smell, too.

Does your dog sniff you?

Your dog remembers how you smell better than it remembers what you look like.

# Why do dogs
# lick people?

Dogs smell through their noses. They also smell through very tiny openings in their mouths behind their top, front teeth.

Licking can help dogs find out who people and other dogs are.

Dogs may also lick people because they like the taste of their salty skin.

# Why do dogs pee so often on a walk?

Dogs pee to leave their own special smell behind. They want other dogs to know they were there. They are also saying, "This place is mine!"

# Why do dogs roll in stinky stuff?

Dogs sometimes like to roll in other animals' poop or in garbage. They do this to cover their own smell.

In the wild, some animals run away if they smell a dog or wolf nearby. Dogs and wolves cover their smell so they can sneak up on other animals.

# Why do dogs pant?

When a dog pants, it breathes hard and fast through its open mouth.

Dogs pant when they are too hot. It helps them cool off.

People sweat to cool off. But dogs cannot sweat through their fur. They lose heat through their tongues instead.

# Why do dogs have bad breath?

Over time, slime forms on a dog's teeth and gums. This can smell bad. Dogs can't brush their teeth. Wouldn't you have bad breath if you never brushed?

# Why do dogs wag their tails?

Dogs wag their tails when they are happy. If a dog's tail is down between its back legs, it is scared or unhappy.

When two dogs meet, their tails show what they are thinking. If their tails stick out straight, they are deciding who is in charge. If one dog's tail is high and the other's is low, the high-tail dog is the boss.

# What other ways do dogs talk with their bodies?

Your dog uses its body to show how it feels and to tell you what it wants.

When your dog rolls onto its back, it may be saying "You are the boss" or "Rub my tummy."

If its tail and ears stand straight up and it shows its teeth, your dog is angry.

When your dog holds out one paw,
it is asking you for something.

If your dog bows down on its
front legs, that usually means it
wants to play.

# What kinds of jobs can dogs do?

Your dog's job is to be your friend. But dogs can do many other jobs. Some bloodhounds help find lost people. Their keen sense of smell also helps them track criminals.

Sheepdogs and collies can herd. They are good at rounding up sheep or cows.

Some huskies pull snow sleds. They have thick, warm fur and lots of energy.

Some German shepherds are trained to be Seeing Eye dogs or police dogs. They are fast learners, very smart, and good at obeying directions.

# What other kinds of jobs can dogs do?

Saint Bernards are good at finding people lost in snowstorms. They have a very strong sense of smell. They can also sense the body heat of a person buried under snow.

Doberman pinschers (say: DO-ber-mun PIN-sherz) can be guard dogs.

They will bark to scare away strangers. Some dogs are actors. They are good at following directions and staying calm. They do not get upset by the lights and noise on a television or movie set.

Scene 1
My Dog
Danny

# Are there any dog heroes?

## Balto

Many dogs have done brave things.

A sled dog named Balto once helped carry medicine to a town in Alaska. He ran for 20 hours in a snowstorm. Without his help, many people would have died.

## Barry

A Saint Bernard named Barry rescued many people lost in snowstorms.

He once saved a small girl who was buried in the snow. He lay down next to her to keep her warm. Then he pulled her to a nearby house.

# Buddy

A German shepherd named Buddy was the first Seeing Eye dog.

Buddy was trained to help a blind man. Buddy helped him cross streets safely.

For the first time, the man could travel and go to work on his own, thanks to Buddy.

# Do dogs understand words?

Experts think some dogs can learn 20 or more words. This helps make dogs easier to train than many other animals.

Most dogs can learn the command words *sit*, *stay*, and *come*.

Dogs may understand many other words.

How many words does your dog know?

good dog —

# Training

When your dog is old enough, you can teach it to obey and do tricks.

Train your dog for only one to five minutes each time.

Teach one trick at a time.

Speak slowly and clearly.

Never hit or shout at your dog.

Always say "good dog" and give your dog a treat, a hug, or a pat when it obeys.

# Training your dog to sit

Hold a small treat over your dog's nose. Move the treat backward over your dog's head. Gently push your dog's rear down until it sits. Each time your dog sits down, say "sit," and give it the treat.

# Training your dog to come

Stand about five steps away from your dog. Look into its eyes for a moment. Then say "come." Use hand movements, too.

Try to teach your dog to sit instead of jumping up when it comes to you.

come

stay

# Training your dog to stay

Hold one hand out with your palm
facing your dog. Say "stay." Keep
your hand out. Step away from your
dog slowly and say "stay" over and
over. If your dog does not stay put,
start again.

Most pet dogs want to be their

owner's best buddy.

Your dog loves you.

Take good care of your dog . . .

and it will be your friend forever.